SHOP DRAWINGS
OF
SHAKER FURNITURE
AND
WOODENWARE

VOLUME II

MEASURED DRAWINGS
BY
EJNER HANDBERG

7.95

THE BERKSHIRE TRAVELLER PRESS
Stockbridge, Massachusetts

BOOKS OF SHAKER INTEREST BY EJNER HANDBERG
FROM BERKSHIRE TRAVELLER PRESS

Shop Drawings of Shaker Furniture and Woodenware,
    Vol. I, Vol. II, Vol. III
Shop Drawings of Shaker Iron and Tinware
Measured Drawings of Shaker Furniture and Woodenware

ALSO BY EJNER HANDBERG:
    Measured Drawings of Eighteenth-Century American Furniture

Photographs by Jane McWhorter

SHOP DRAWINGS OF SHAKER FURNITURE AND WOODENWARE, VOL. II.
Copyright © 1975 by Ejner P. Handberg. All rights reserved. No part of this book may be used or reproduced in any manner whatsoever without written permission. For information address The Berkshire Traveller Press, Stockbridge, MA 01262.

ISBN 0-912944-29-3
Library of Congress No. 73-83797

Printed in the United States of America by Studley Press, Dalton, MA 01226

20   19   18   17   16   15

ACKNOWLEDGMENTS

This second book of "Shaker Drawings" includes pieces of Shaker furniture which have been in my shop as well as several other interesting pieces from collections mentioned below.

Special thanks are due Mrs. Edward Deming Andrews for permission to make measured drawings of several more pieces from the Andrews collection and for the help and information given me.

I am also very grateful for the cooperation and for similar help and permission at Hancock Shaker Village, Hancock, Massachusetts and the Shaker Museum, Old Chatham, New York.

Although the Shaker cabinetmakers were obliged to make their furniture and woodenware with utility in mind, their work is eagerly sought today by museums and private collectors for its simplicity and beauty. I wish to thank several of these collectors for allowing me to examine and make drawings of Shaker pieces in their possession.

E. H.

CONTENTS

NOTES TO THE CRAFTSMAN OR COLLECTOR

White pine was the most common wood used for furniture like cupboards, chests of drawers, benches, woodboxes and many other items.

Bedposts, chairposts and all parts requiring strength were usually made of hard maple or yellow birch.

Maple, birch and cherry were used for legs on trestle tables, drop leaf tables and stands. The tops were often pine. Square legs are tapered on the inner surfaces only.

Sometimes candlestands, work stands and sewing stands were made entirely of cherry, maple or birch. The legs are dovetailed to the shaft and the grain should run as nearly parallel to the general direction of the leg as possible. A thin metal plate should be fastened to the underside of the shaft and extend about three quarters of an inch along the base of each leg with a screw or nail put in the leg to keep them from spreading.

Parts for chairs and stools were mostly hard maple with an occasional chair made of curly or bird's-eye maple. Birch, cherry and butternut were used less often.

Oval boxes and carriers were nearly always made of maple. The bottoms and covers were fitted with quarter-sawn, edge-grain pine which is less apt to cup or warp than flat-grained boards. First the "fingers" or "lappers" are cut on the maple bands, then they are steamed and wrapped around an oval form and the fingers fastened with small copper or iron rivets (tacks). After they are dry and sanded the pine disks are fitted into the bottom and cover and fastened with small square copper or iron brads.

In New York State and New England, the woods used for the many different small pieces of cabinet work and woodenware were white pine, maple, cherry, yellow birch, butternut and native walnut. They were often finished with a coat of thin paint, or stained and varnished, or sometimes left with a natural finish.

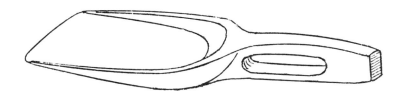

"BEAUTY RESTS ON UTILITY"

WALL CLOCK
BY I. N. YOUNGS
HANCOCK SHAKER VILLAGE, HANCOCK MASS.

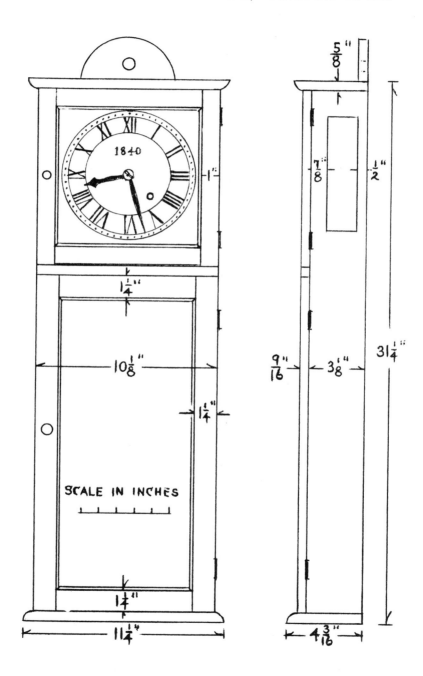

SCALE IN INCHES

WALL CLOCK
BY I. N. YOUNGS
HANCOCK SHAKER VILLAGE, HANCOCK MASS.

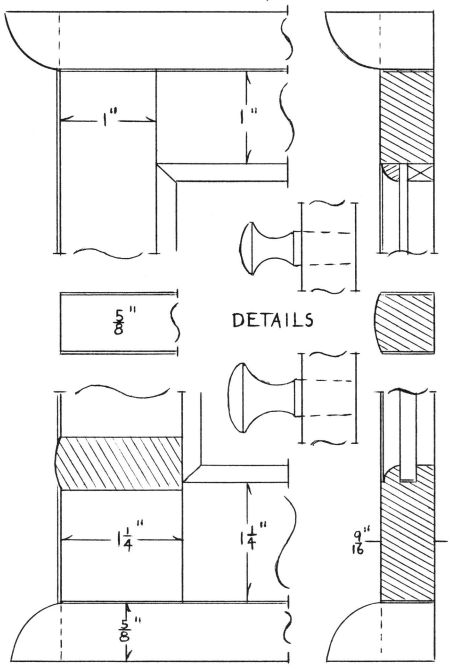

DETAILS

DESK
CHERRY

FROM ANDREWS
COLLECTION

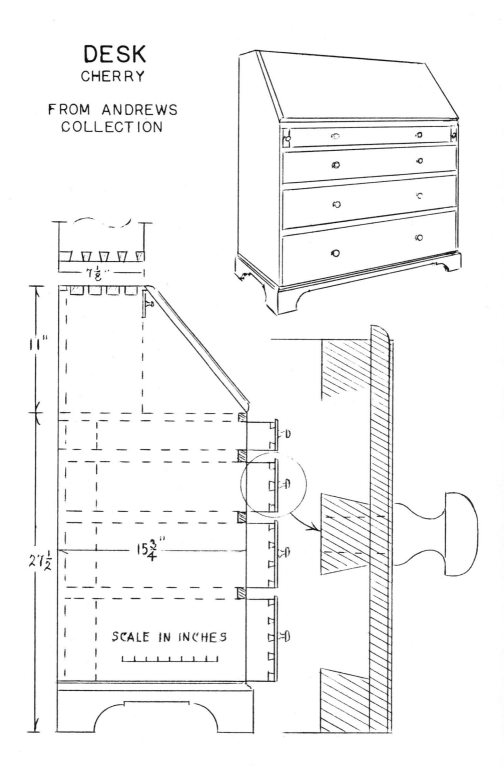

$7\frac{1}{8}''$

$11''$

$15\frac{3}{4}''$

$27\frac{1}{2}''$

SCALE IN INCHES

DESK
CHERRY

LIP
ONLY ON TOP

FROM
ANDREWS
COLLECTION

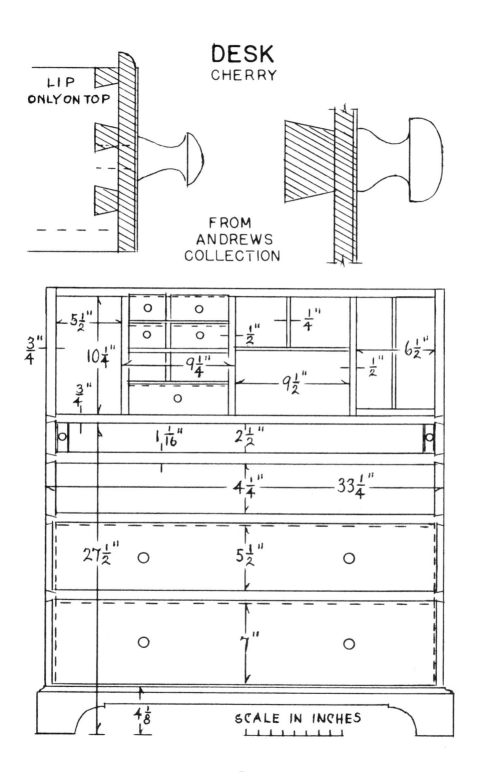

SCALE IN INCHES

5

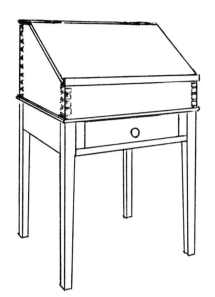

PINE DESK

THE SHAKER MUSEUM,
OLD CHATHAM, N.Y.

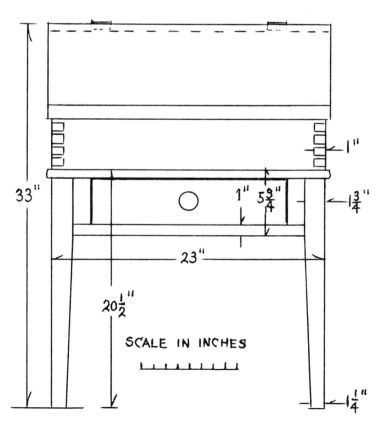

1"

33"

1" 5¾"

1¾"

23"

20½"

SCALE IN INCHES

1¼"

6

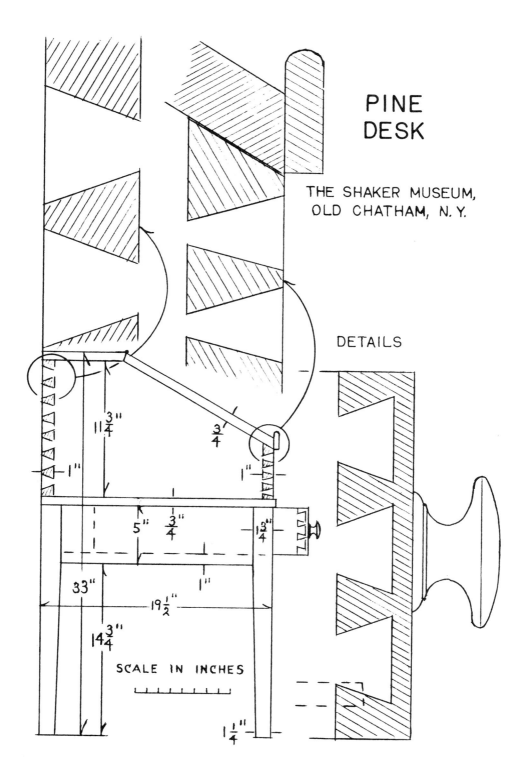

PINE
DESK

THE SHAKER MUSEUM,
OLD CHATHAM, N.Y.

DETAILS

$11\frac{3}{4}$"

$\frac{3}{4}$"

1"

5" $\frac{3}{4}$"

$1\frac{3}{4}$"

1"

33"

$19\frac{1}{2}$"

$14\frac{3}{4}$"

SCALE IN INCHES

$1\frac{1}{4}$"

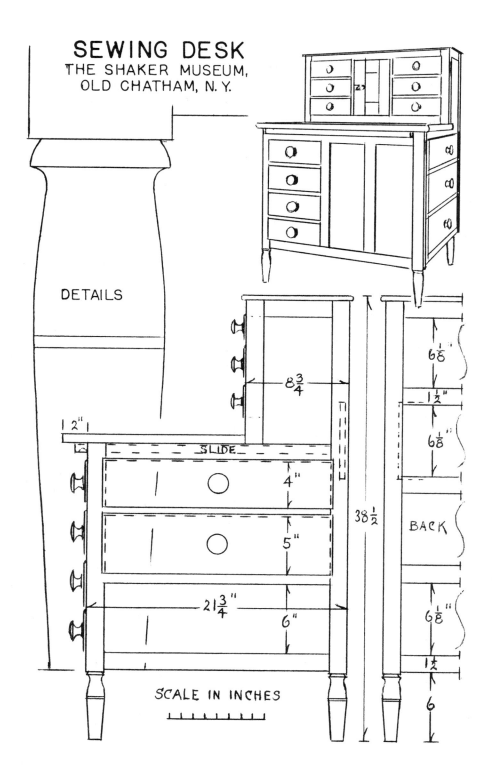

SEWING DESK
THE SHAKER MUSEUM,
OLD CHATHAM, N.Y.

DETAILS

2"

8$\frac{3}{4}$

SLIDE

4"

5"

21$\frac{3}{4}$"

6"

38$\frac{1}{2}$

6$\frac{1}{8}$

1$\frac{1}{2}$"

6$\frac{1}{8}$"

BACK

6$\frac{1}{8}$"

1$\frac{1}{2}$

6

SCALE IN INCHES

SEWING DESK
THE SHAKER MUSEUM, OLD CHATHAM, N.Y.

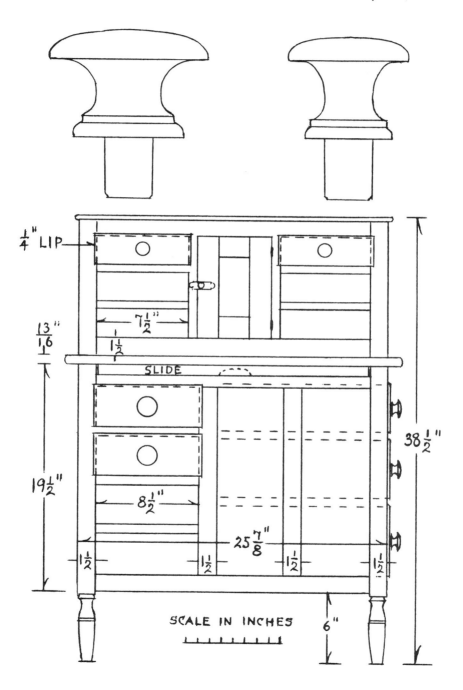

$\frac{1}{4}$" LIP

$\frac{13}{16}$"

$7\frac{1}{2}$"

$1\frac{1}{2}$

SLIDE

$19\frac{1}{2}$"

$8\frac{1}{2}$"

$1\frac{1}{2}$

$25\frac{7}{8}$"

$1\frac{1}{2}$

$1\frac{1}{2}$

$1\frac{1}{2}$

$38\frac{1}{2}$"

SCALE IN INCHES

6"

PINE
SEWING DESK

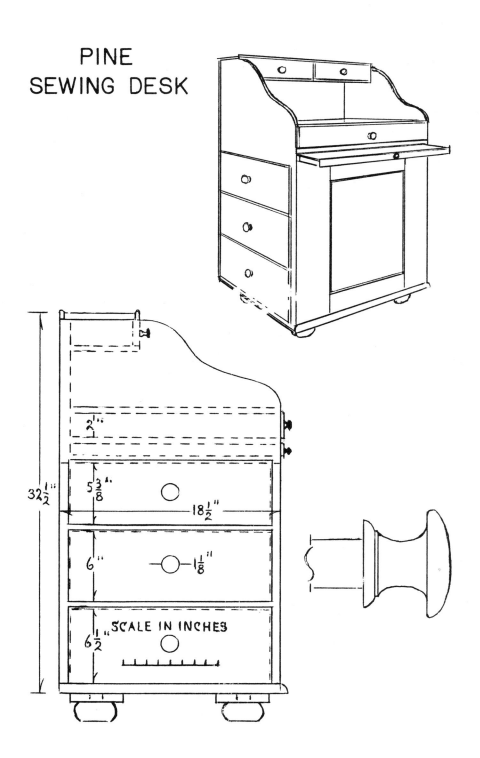

SCALE IN INCHES

PINE SEWING DESK

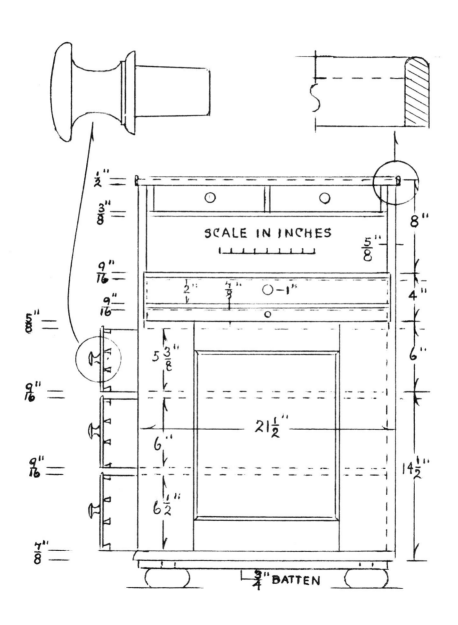

SCALE IN INCHES

$\frac{3}{4}$" BATTEN

SEWING TABLE
THE SHAKER MUSEUM, OLD CHATHAM, N.Y.
CHERRY WITH PINE TOP

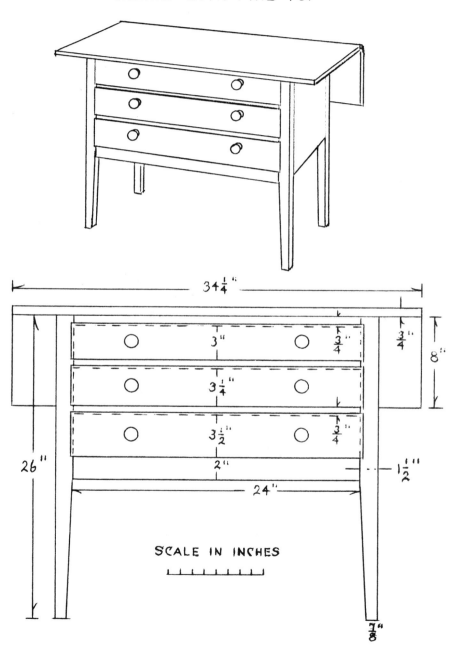

SCALE IN INCHES

SEWING TABLE

THE SHAKER MUSEUM, OLD CHATHAM, N. Y.

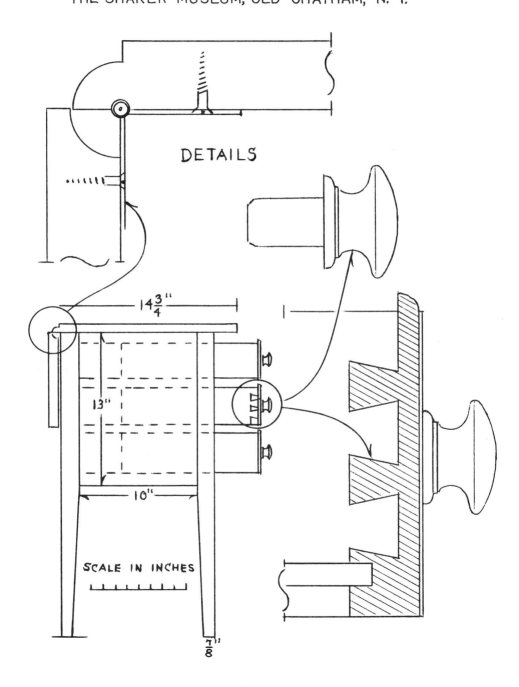

DETAILS

$14\frac{3}{4}$"

13"

10"

SCALE IN INCHES

$\frac{7}{8}$"

PINE TABLE
STAINED RED
FROM ANDREWS COLLECTION

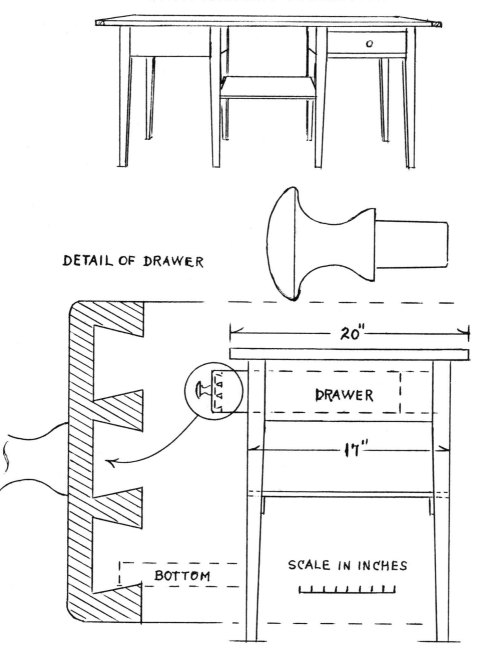

DETAIL OF DRAWER

20"

DRAWER

17"

BOTTOM

SCALE IN INCHES

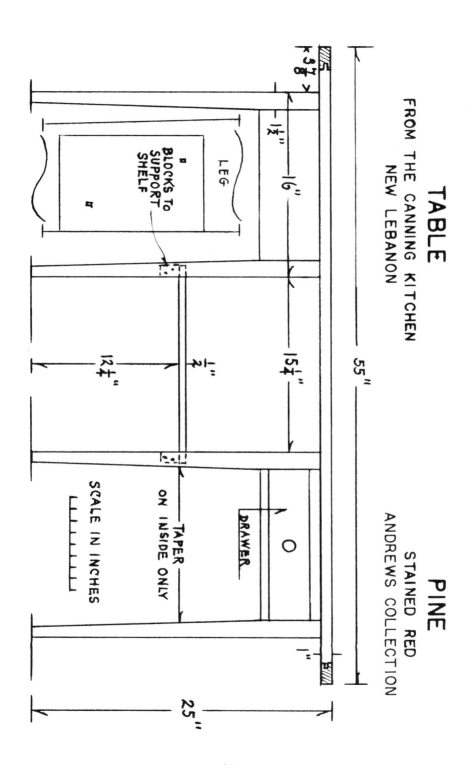

TABLE

FROM THE CANNING KITCHEN
NEW LEBANON

PINE
STAINED RED
ANDREWS COLLECTION

BLOCKS TO
SUPPORT
SHELF

LEG

55"

15¼"

16"

3⅞

1½"

12¼"

½"

TAPER
ON INSIDE ONLY

DRAWER

SCALE IN INCHES

25"

1"

15

BAKE-ROOM TABLE

FROM ANDREWS COLLECTION

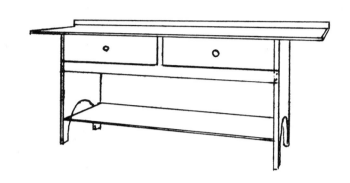

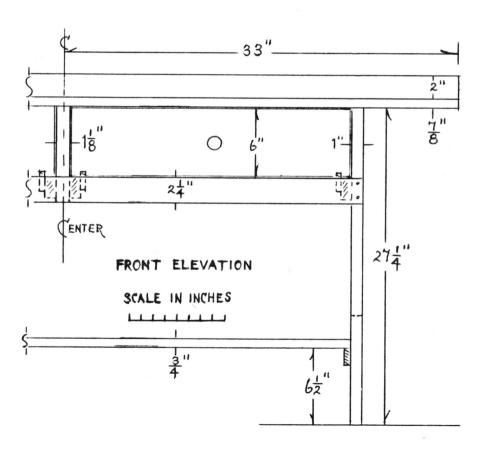

33"

2"

$1\frac{1}{8}$"

6"

1"

$\frac{7}{8}$"

$2\frac{1}{4}$"

CENTER

FRONT ELEVATION

SCALE IN INCHES

$27\frac{1}{4}$"

$\frac{3}{4}$"

$6\frac{1}{2}$"

BAKE-ROOM TABLE
FROM ANDREWS COLLECTION

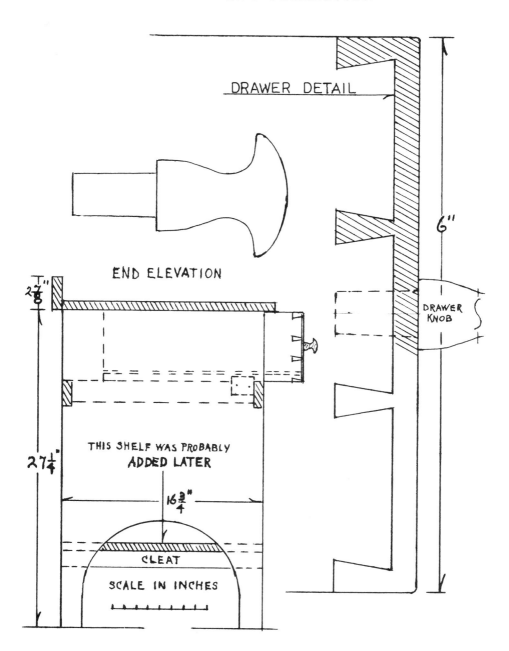

DRAWER DETAIL

END ELEVATION

6"

DRAWER KNOB

$2\frac{7}{8}$"

$27\frac{1}{4}$"

THIS SHELF WAS PROBABLY ADDED LATER

$16\frac{3}{4}$"

CLEAT

SCALE IN INCHES

DROP-LEAF TABLE

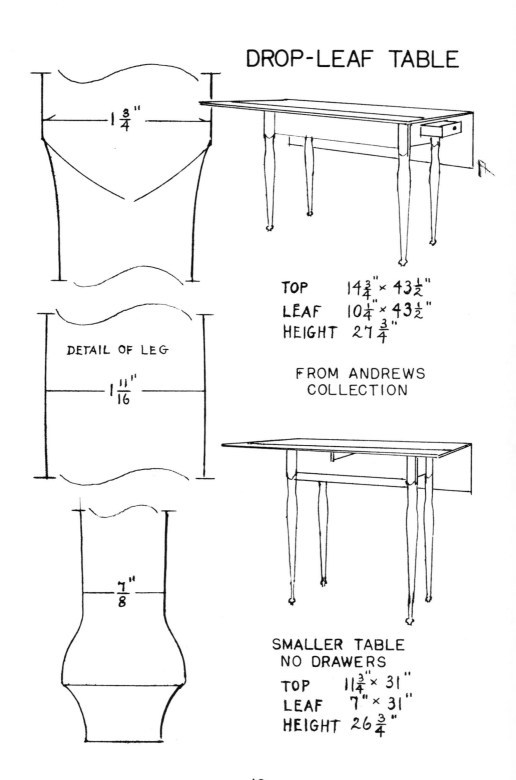

$1\frac{3}{4}$"

DETAIL OF LEG

$1\frac{11}{16}$"

$\frac{7}{8}$"

TOP $14\frac{3}{4}$" × $43\frac{1}{2}$"
LEAF $10\frac{1}{4}$" × $43\frac{1}{2}$"
HEIGHT $27\frac{3}{4}$"

FROM ANDREWS
COLLECTION

SMALLER TABLE
NO DRAWERS
TOP $11\frac{3}{4}$" × 31"
LEAF   7" × 31"
HEIGHT $26\frac{3}{4}$"

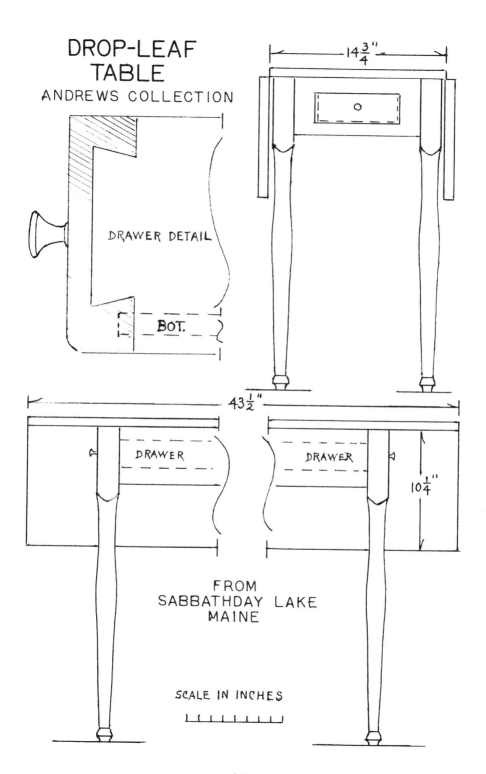

DROP-LEAF
TABLE
ANDREWS COLLECTION

14¾"

DRAWER DETAIL

BOT.

43½"

DRAWER

DRAWER

10¼"

FROM
SABBATHDAY LAKE
MAINE

SCALE IN INCHES

19

SMALL TABLE
LEGS OF CHERRY
TOP, FRAME AND DRAWER OF CHESTNUT

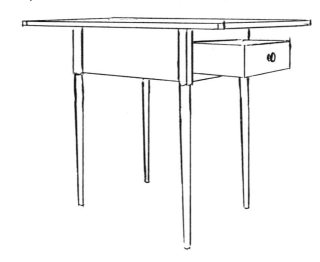

FROM ANDREWS COLLECTION

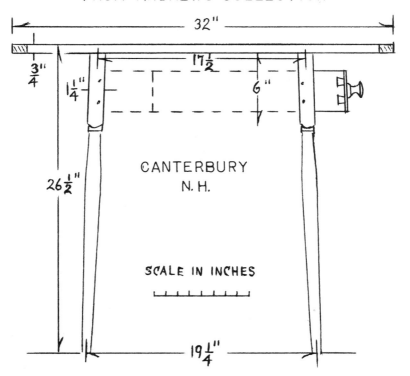

32"

$\frac{3}{4}$"

17$\frac{1}{2}$

1$\frac{1}{4}$"

6"

26$\frac{1}{2}$"

CANTERBURY
N. H.

SCALE IN INCHES

19$\frac{1}{4}$"

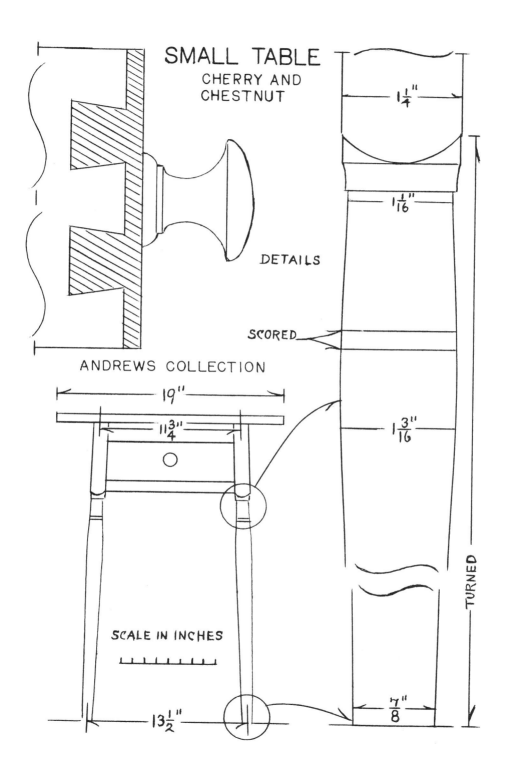

SMALL TABLE
CHERRY AND CHESTNUT

DETAILS

ANDREWS COLLECTION

SCALE IN INCHES

SCORED

TURNED

$1\frac{1}{4}$"

$1\frac{1}{16}$"

$1\frac{3}{16}$"

$\frac{7}{8}$"

19"

$11\frac{3}{4}$"

$13\frac{1}{2}$"

TABLE·
BIRD'S-EYE MAPLE
THE SHAKER MUSEUM,
OLD CHATHAM, N.Y.

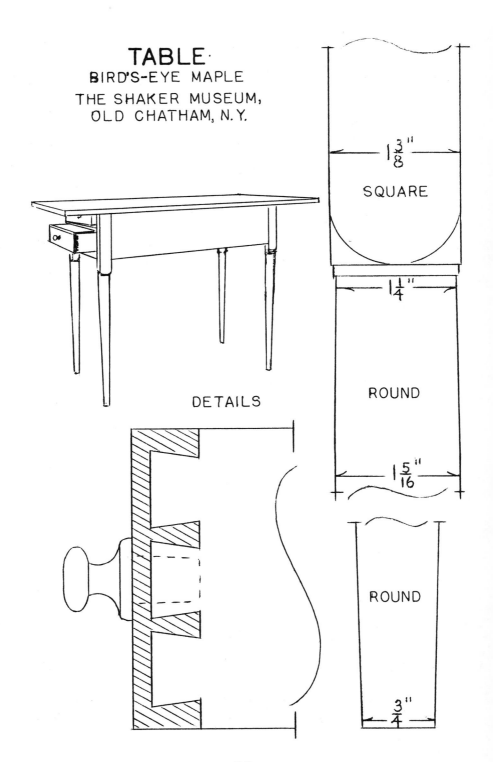

$1\frac{3}{8}"$

SQUARE

$1\frac{1}{4}"$

ROUND

$1\frac{5}{16}"$

ROUND

$\frac{3}{4}"$

DETAILS

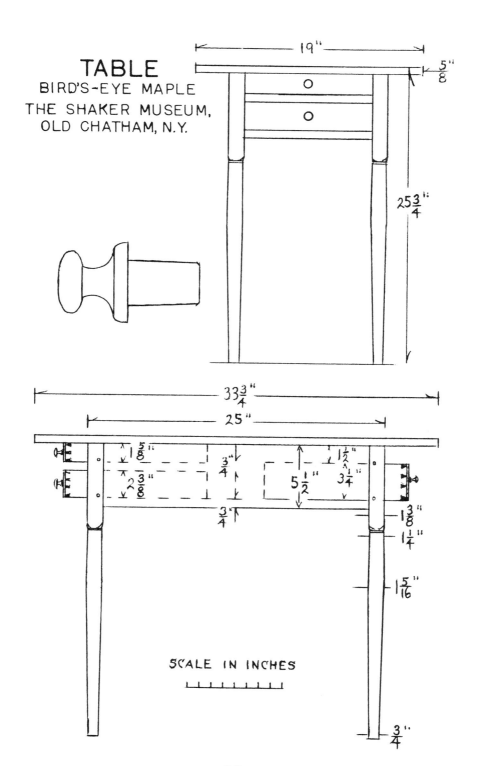

TABLE
BIRD'S-EYE MAPLE
THE SHAKER MUSEUM,
OLD CHATHAM, N.Y.

19"

$\frac{5}{8}$"

$25\frac{3}{4}$"

$33\frac{3}{4}$"

25"

$1\frac{5}{8}$"

$2\frac{3}{8}$"

$\frac{3}{4}$"

$\frac{3}{4}$"

$1\frac{1}{2}$"

$5\frac{1}{2}$"

$3\frac{1}{4}$"

$1\frac{3}{8}$"

$1\frac{1}{4}$"

$1\frac{5}{16}$"

$\frac{3}{4}$"

SCALE IN INCHES

PEG-LEG STAND

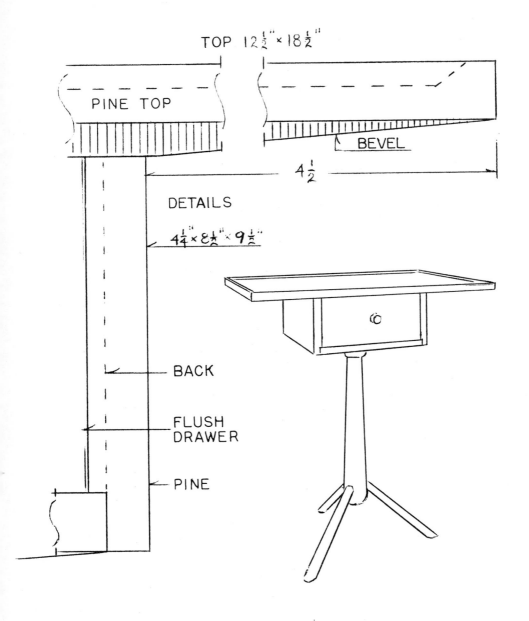

TOP $12\frac{1}{2}" \times 18\frac{1}{2}"$

PINE TOP

BEVEL

$4\frac{1}{2}$

DETAILS

$4\frac{1}{4}" \times 8\frac{1}{2}" \times 9\frac{1}{2}"$

BACK

FLUSH
DRAWER

PINE

PEG-LEG STAND

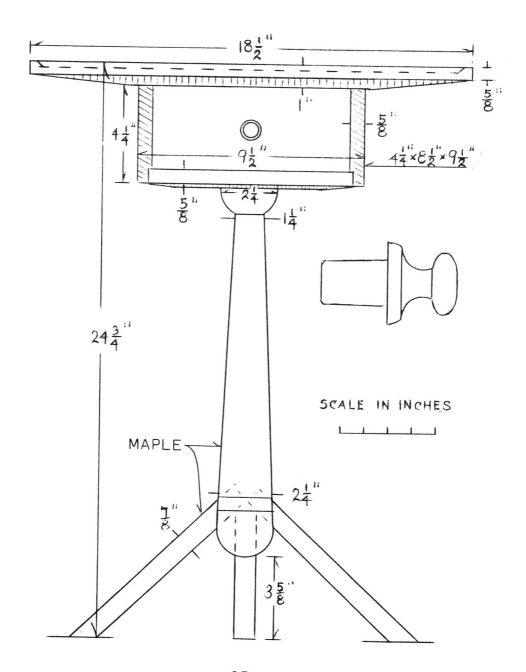

$18\frac{1}{2}"$

$\frac{1}{5}"$

$\frac{1}{8}"$

$1"$

$4\frac{1}{4}"$

$\frac{5}{8}"$

$9\frac{1}{2}"$

$4\frac{1}{4}" \times 8\frac{1}{2}" \times 9\frac{1}{2}"$

$\frac{5}{8}"$

$2\frac{1}{4}"$

$1\frac{1}{4}"$

$24\frac{3}{4}"$

MAPLE

$2\frac{1}{4}"$

$3\frac{1}{4}"$

$3\frac{5}{8}"$

SCALE IN INCHES

DETAIL OF SHAFT

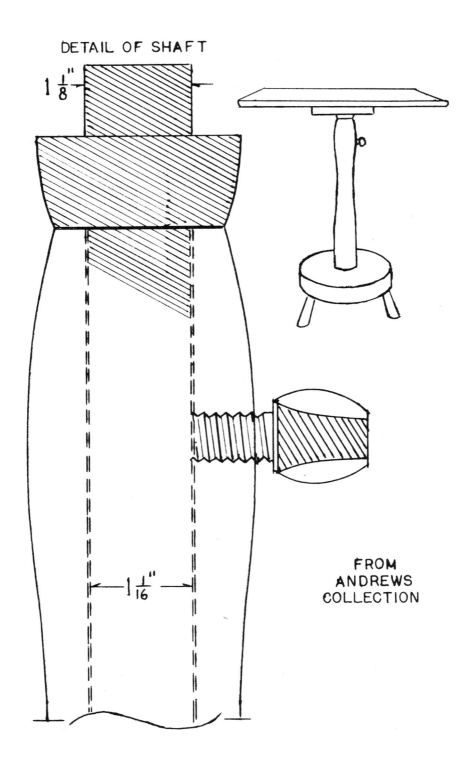

$1\frac{1}{8}"$

$1\frac{1}{16}"$

26

EARLY STAND
WITH ADJUSTABLE TOP

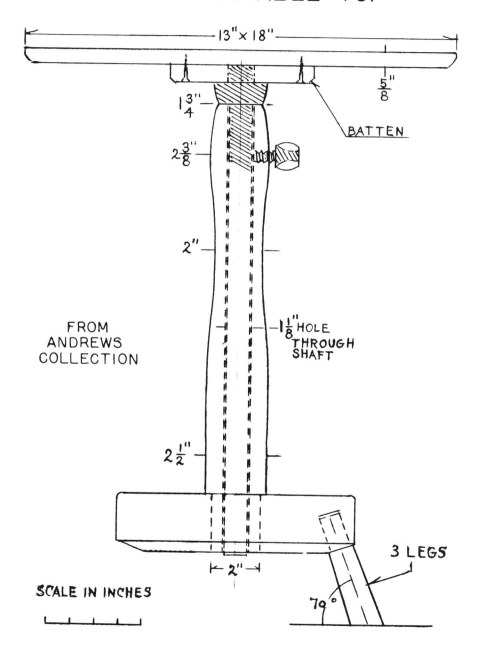

13" × 18"

$\frac{5}{8}$"

$1\frac{3}{4}$"

BATTEN

$2\frac{3}{8}$"

2"

FROM
ANDREWS
COLLECTION

$1\frac{1}{8}$" HOLE
THROUGH
SHAFT

$2\frac{1}{2}$"

3 LEGS

2"

SCALE IN INCHES

79°

STAND WITH ADJUSTABLE TOP
MAPLE AND PINE

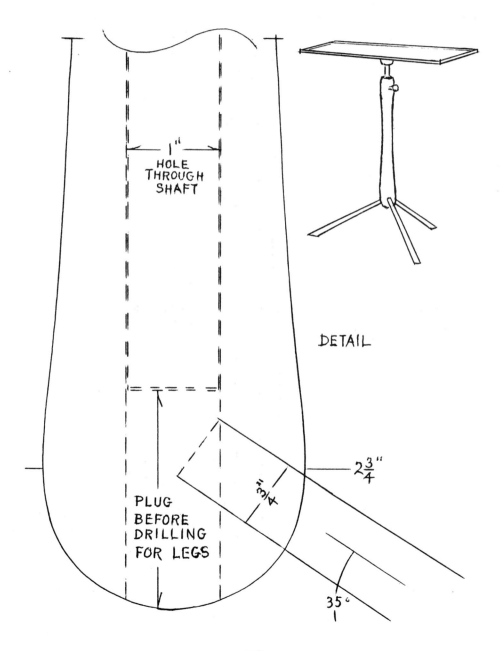

1" HOLE THROUGH SHAFT

DETAIL

PLUG BEFORE DRILLING FOR LEGS

$2\frac{3}{4}$"

$\frac{3}{4}$"

35°

STAND WITH ADJUSTABLE TOP
SHAFT AND LEGS OF MAPLE TOP OF PINE

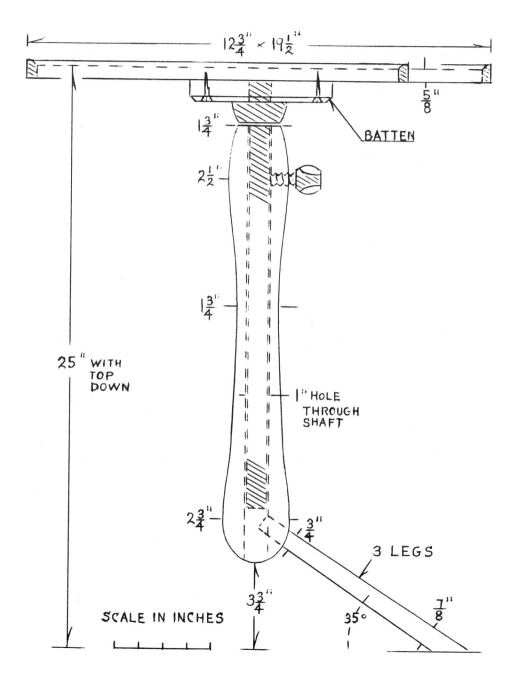

$12\frac{3}{4}" \times 19\frac{1}{2}"$

$\frac{5}{8}"$

BATTEN

$1\frac{3}{4}"$

$2\frac{1}{2}"$

$1\frac{3}{4}"$

25" WITH TOP DOWN

1" HOLE THROUGH SHAFT

$2\frac{3}{4}"$

$\frac{3}{4}"$

3 LEGS

$3\frac{3}{4}"$

35°

$\frac{7}{8}"$

SCALE IN INCHES

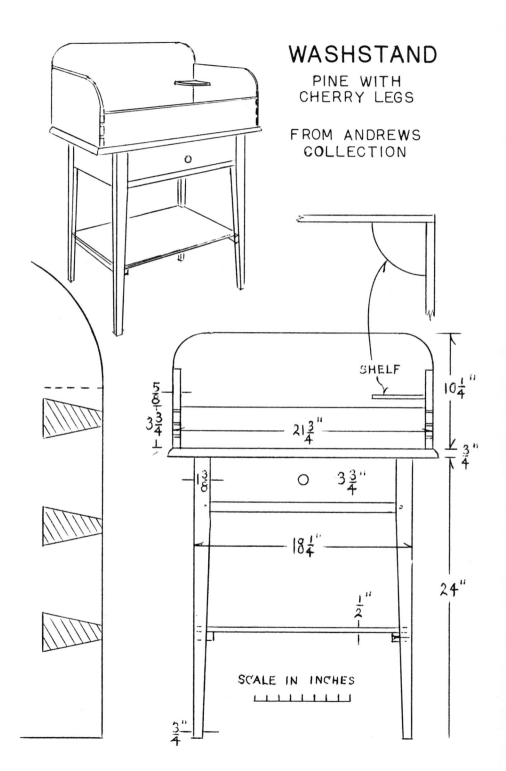

WASHSTAND

PINE WITH CHERRY LEGS

FROM ANDREWS COLLECTION

SHELF

$10\frac{1}{4}''$

$21\frac{3}{4}''$

$3\frac{3}{4}''$

$10\frac{5}{8}''$

$\frac{3}{4}''$

$1\frac{3}{8}''$

$3\frac{3}{4}''$

$18\frac{1}{4}''$

$\frac{1}{2}''$

$24''$

SCALE IN INCHES

$\frac{3}{4}''$

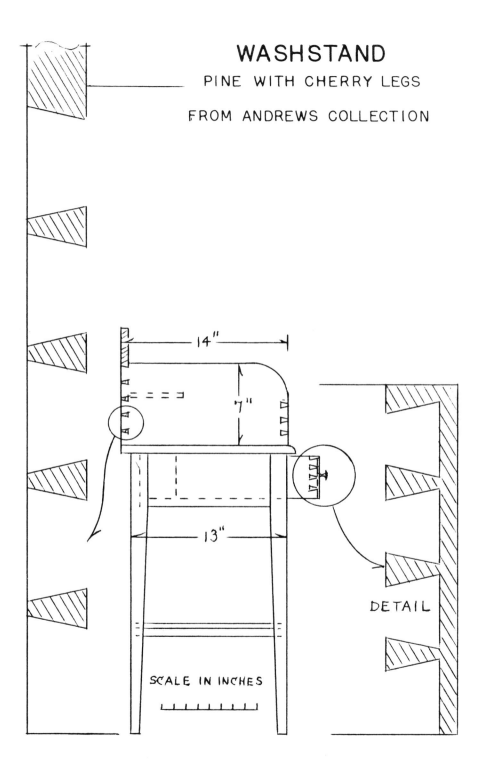

WASHSTAND

PINE WITH CHERRY LEGS

FROM ANDREWS COLLECTION

14"

7"

13"

DETAIL

SCALE IN INCHES

31

WASHSTAND

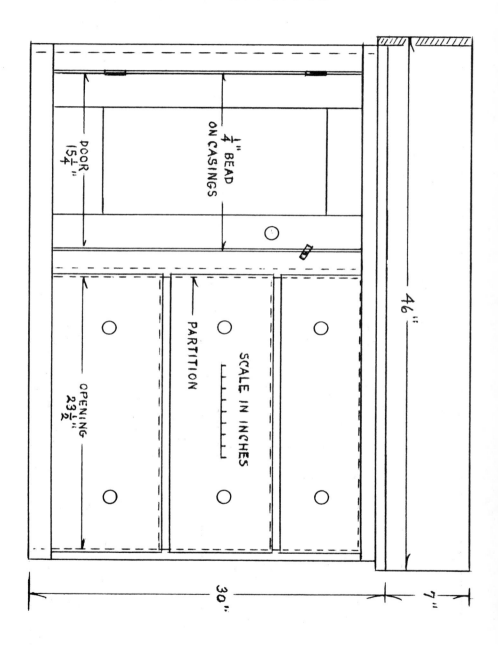

DOOR
15¼"

¼" BEAD
ON CASINGS

OPENING
23½"

PARTITION

SCALE IN INCHES

46"

30"

7"

FROM ANDREWS COLLECTION

32

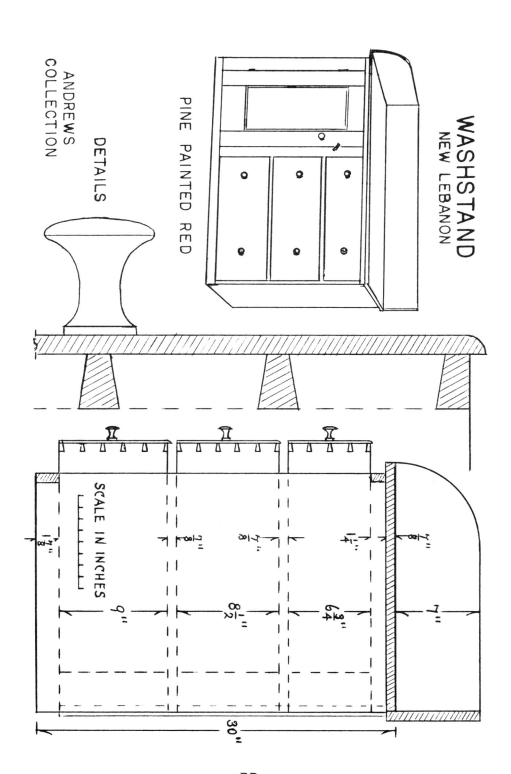

WASHSTAND
NEW LEBANON

ANDREWS
COLLECTION

DETAILS

PINE PAINTED RED

SCALE IN INCHES

$\frac{7}{8}$"

$\frac{7}{8}$"

$\frac{7}{8}$"

1$\frac{1}{4}$"

1$\frac{1}{4}$"

9"

8$\frac{1}{2}$"

6$\frac{3}{64}$"

7"

30"

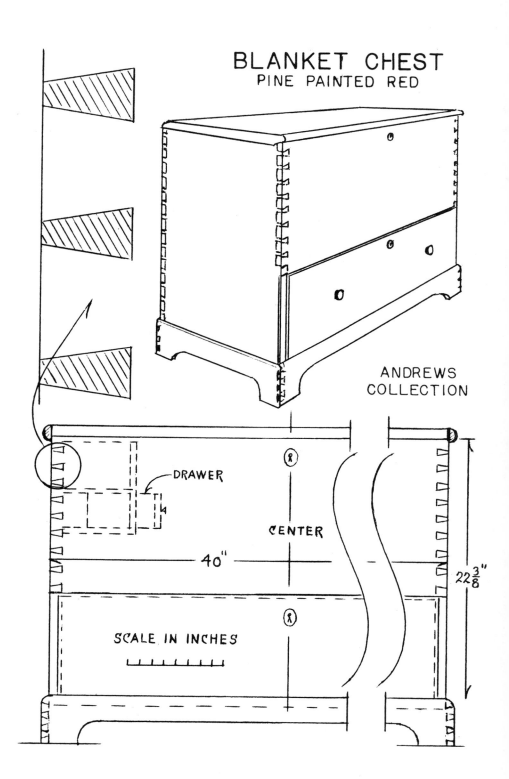

BLANKET CHEST
PINE PAINTED RED

ANDREWS
COLLECTION

DRAWER

CENTER

40"

$22\frac{3}{8}$"

SCALE IN INCHES

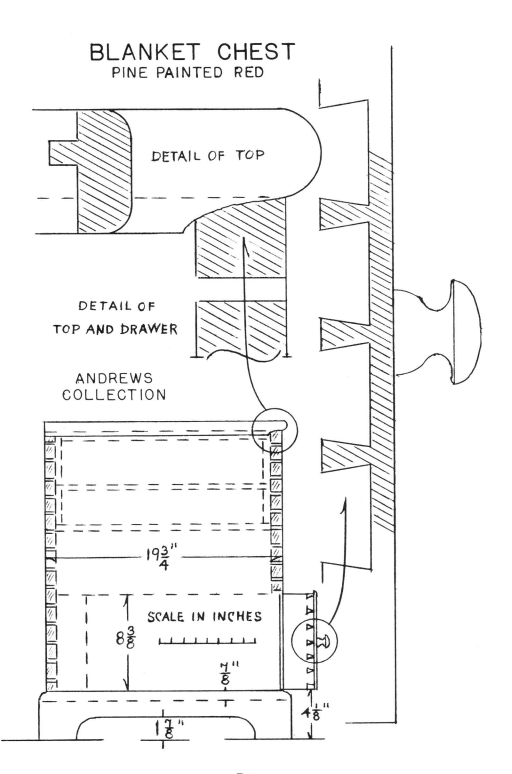

BLANKET CHEST
PINE PAINTED RED

DETAIL OF TOP

DETAIL OF
TOP AND DRAWER

ANDREWS
COLLECTION

$19\frac{3}{4}''$

SCALE IN INCHES

$8\frac{3}{8}$

$\frac{7}{8}''$

$4\frac{1}{8}''$

$1\frac{7}{8}''$

WOOD-BOX
PINE, STAINED RED

FROM
ANDREWS
COLLECTION

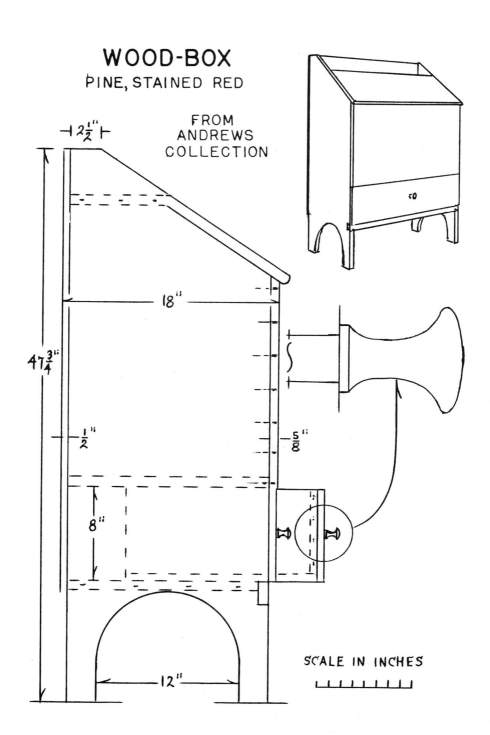

$2\frac{1}{2}"$

18"

$47\frac{3}{4}"$

$\frac{1}{2}"$

$\frac{5}{8}"$

8"

12"

SCALE IN INCHES

WOOD-BOX

MADE FOR THE MINISTRY CANTERBURY N.H.

FROM ANDREWS COLLECTION

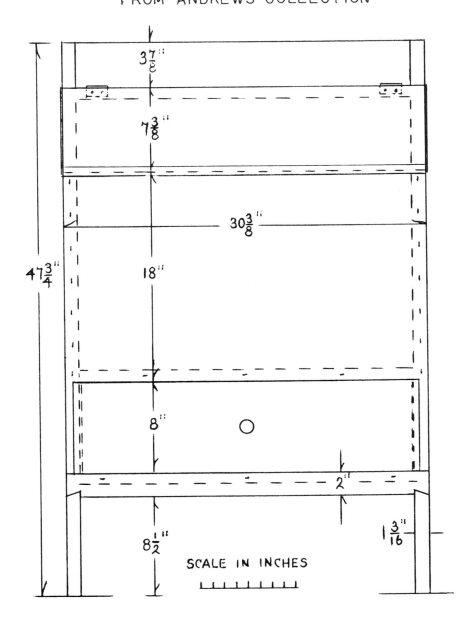

SCALE IN INCHES

2 DRAWER UTILITY CHEST

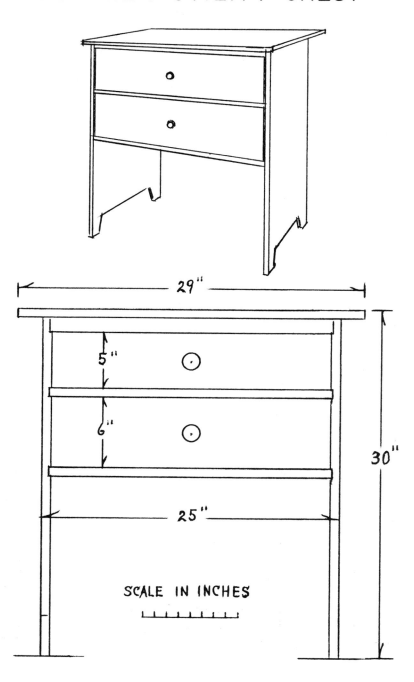

29"

5"

6"

30"

25"

SCALE IN INCHES

2 DRAWER UTILITY CHEST
FROM ANDREWS COLLECTION

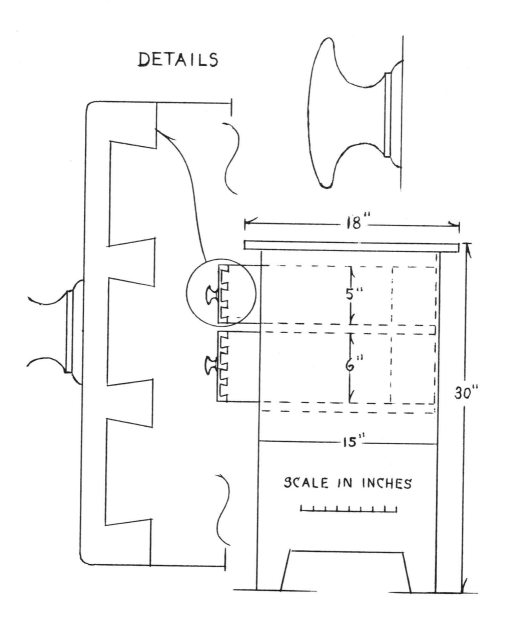

DETAILS

18"

5"

6"

30"

15"

SCALE IN INCHES

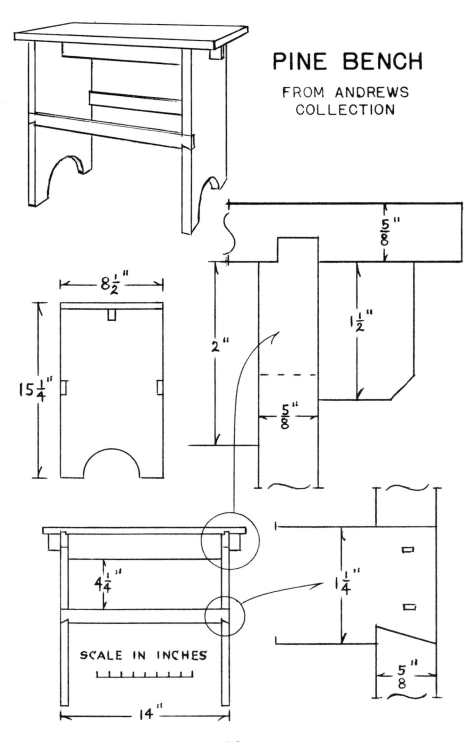

PINE BENCH

FROM ANDREWS
COLLECTION

$\frac{5}{8}$"

$8\frac{1}{2}$"

$1\frac{1}{2}$"

$15\frac{1}{4}$"

2"

$\frac{5}{8}$"

$4\frac{1}{4}$"

$1\frac{1}{4}$"

SCALE IN INCHES

$\frac{5}{8}$"

14"

40

KITCHEN BENCH
HANCOCK SHAKER VILLAGE, HANCOCK MASS.

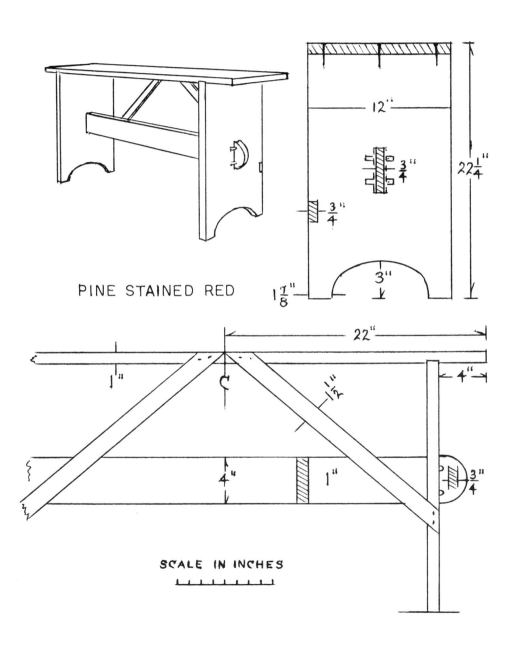

PINE STAINED RED

12"

22$\frac{1}{4}$"

$\frac{3}{4}$"

$\frac{3}{4}$"

3"

1$\frac{7}{8}$"

22"

1"

$\frac{1}{2}$"

4"

4"

1"

$\frac{3}{4}$"

SCALE IN INCHES

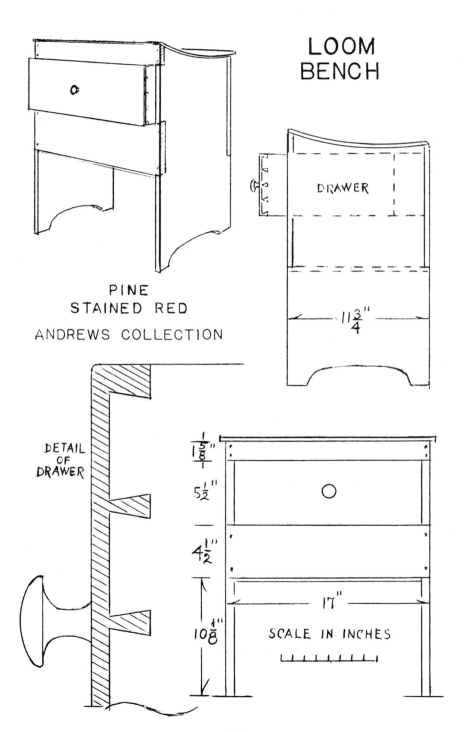

LOOM
BENCH

PINE
STAINED RED

ANDREWS COLLECTION

DRAWER

$11\frac{3}{4}$"

DETAIL
OF
DRAWER

$1\frac{5}{8}$"

$5\frac{1}{2}$"

$4\frac{1}{2}$"

17"

$10\frac{1}{8}$"

SCALE IN INCHES

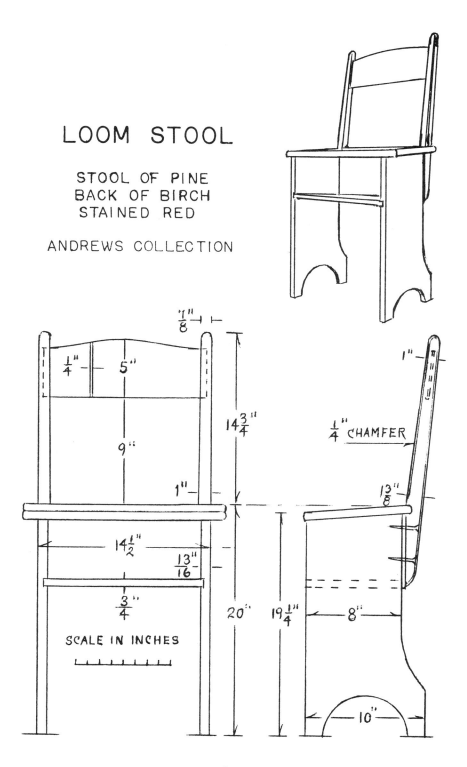

LOOM STOOL

STOOL OF PINE
BACK OF BIRCH
STAINED RED

ANDREWS COLLECTION

SCALE IN INCHES

¼" CHAMFER

43

STEP-STOOL

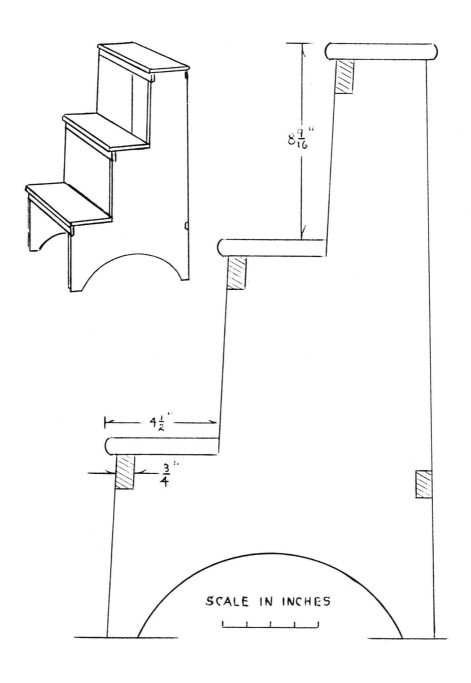

$8\frac{9}{16}$"

$4\frac{1}{2}$"

$\frac{3}{4}$"

SCALE IN INCHES

STEP-STOOL

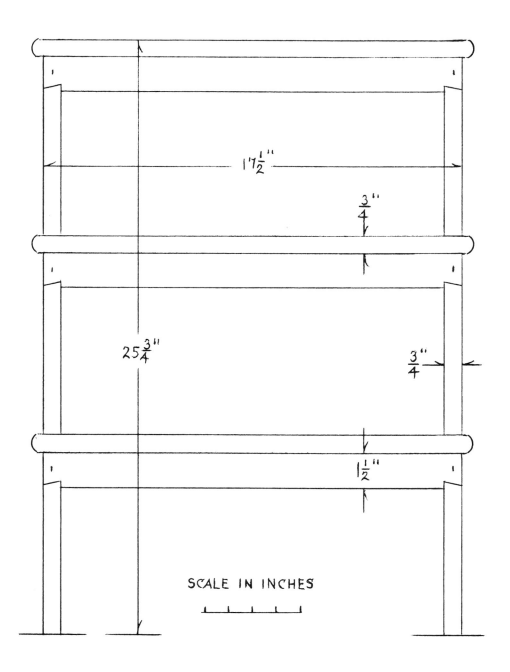

$17\frac{1}{2}''$

$\frac{3}{4}''$

$25\frac{3}{4}''$

$\frac{3}{4}''$

$1\frac{1}{2}''$

SCALE IN INCHES

REVOLVING STOOL

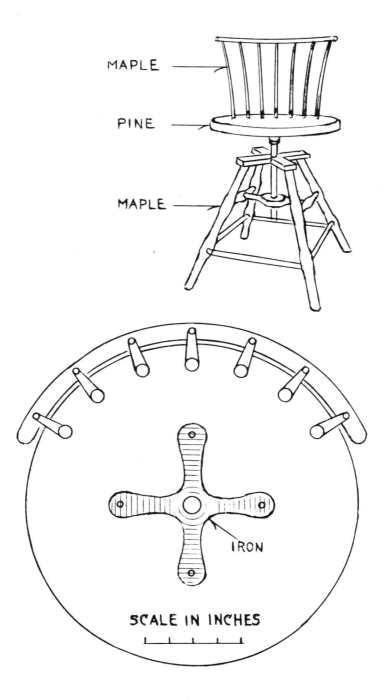

MAPLE

PINE

MAPLE

IRON

SCALE IN INCHES

REVOLVING STOOL

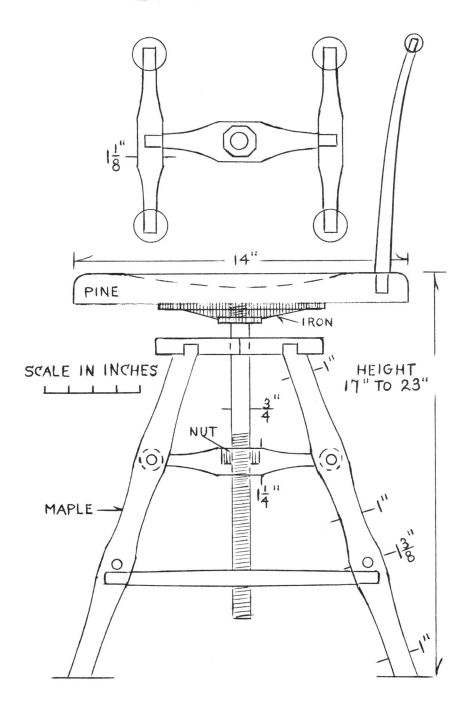

$1\frac{1}{8}$"

14"

PINE

IRON

SCALE IN INCHES

HEIGHT
17" TO 23"

$\frac{3}{4}$"

NUT

1"

$1\frac{1}{4}$"

MAPLE

1"

$1\frac{3}{8}$"

1"

STOOL MT. LEBANON

THE SHAKER MUSEUM
OLD CHATHAM, N.Y.

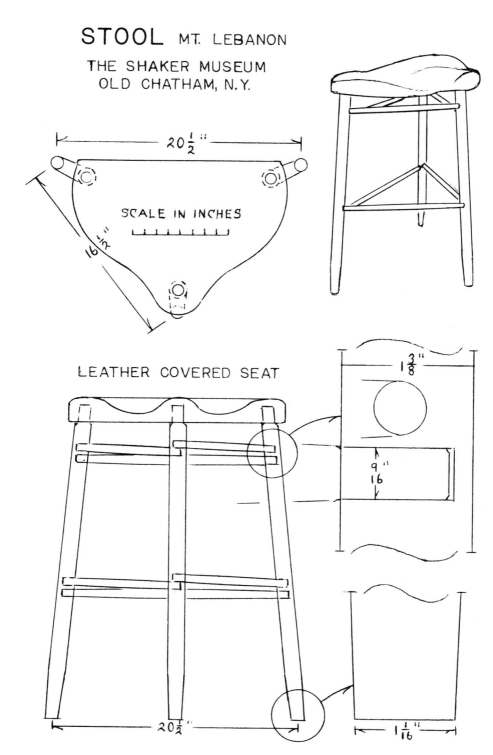

$20\frac{1}{2}''$

SCALE IN INCHES

$16\frac{1}{2}''$

LEATHER COVERED SEAT

$1\frac{3}{8}''$

$\frac{9}{16}''$

$20\frac{1}{2}''$

$1\frac{1}{16}''$

STOOL

THE SHAKER MUSEUM, OLD CHATHAM, N.Y.

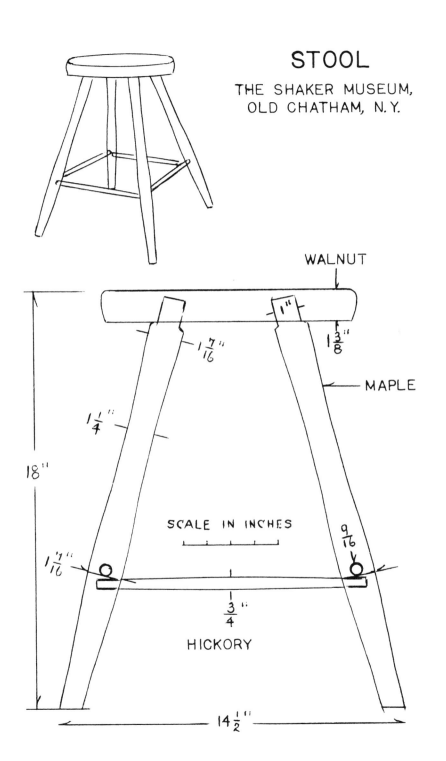

WALNUT

1"

1 3/8"

1 7/16"

MAPLE

1 1/4"

18"

SCALE IN INCHES

9/16

1 1/16"

3/4"

HICKORY

14 1/2"

ELDER ROBERT M. WAGAN
CHAIRMAKER

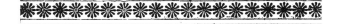

Illustrated Catalogue

AND

PRICE LIST

OF

Shakers' ❖ Chairs,

MANUFACTURED BY THE

Society ❋ of ❋ Shakers.

R. M. WAGAN & CO,

MOUNT LEBANON, N. Y.

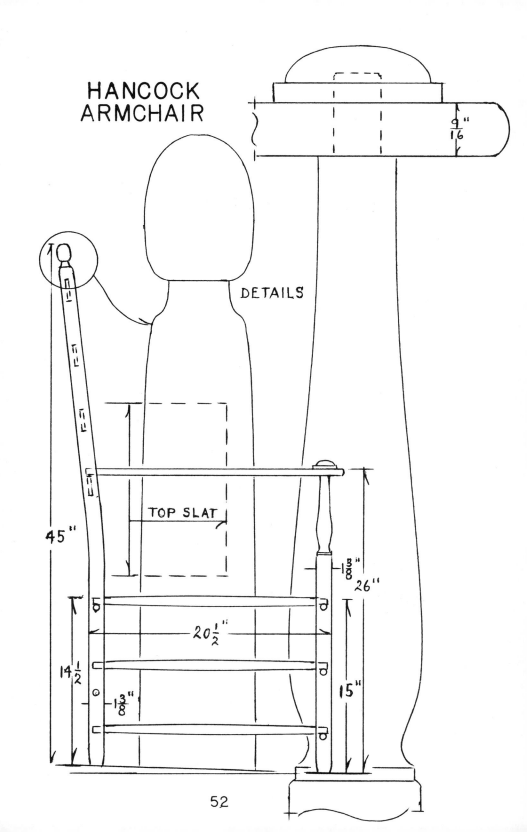

HANCOCK
ARMCHAIR

DETAILS

TOP SLAT

45"

20½"

14½"

1⅜"

1⅜"

9/16"

26"

15"

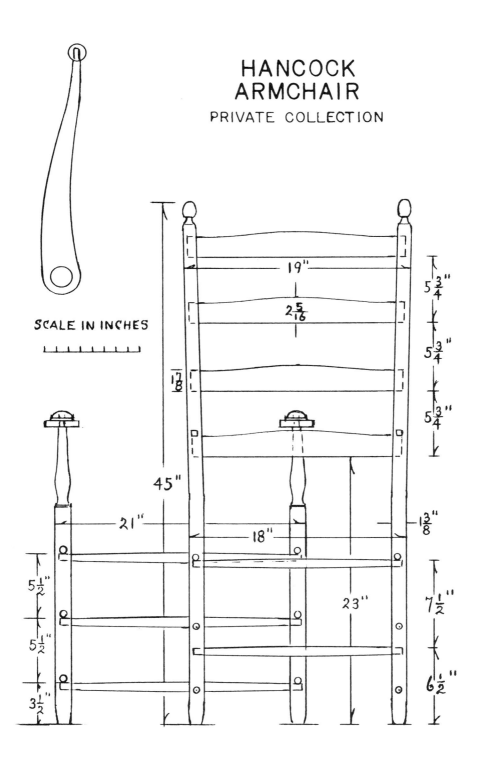

HANCOCK
ARMCHAIR
PRIVATE COLLECTION

SCALE IN INCHES

19"

$5\frac{3}{4}$"

$2\frac{5}{16}$

$5\frac{3}{4}$"

$5\frac{3}{4}$"

$1\frac{7}{8}$

45"

21"

18"

$1\frac{3}{8}$"

$5\frac{1}{2}$"

23"

$7\frac{1}{2}$"

$5\frac{1}{2}$"

$3\frac{1}{2}$"

$6\frac{1}{2}$"

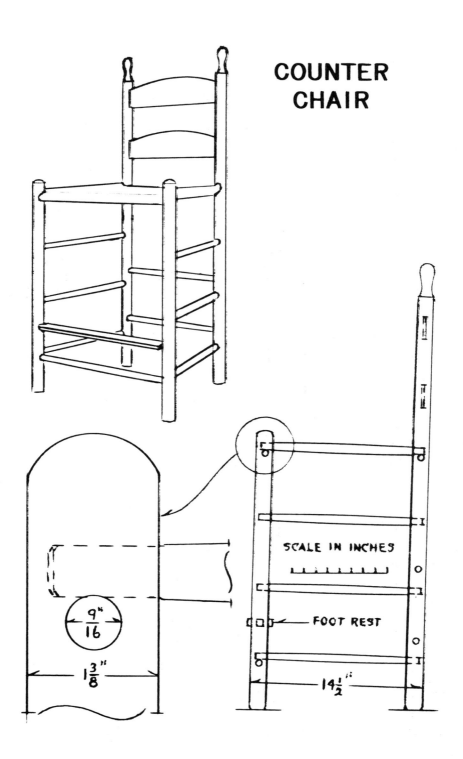

COUNTER
CHAIR

SCALE IN INCHES

FOOT REST

$\frac{9''}{16}$

$1\frac{3}{8}''$

$14\frac{1}{2}''$

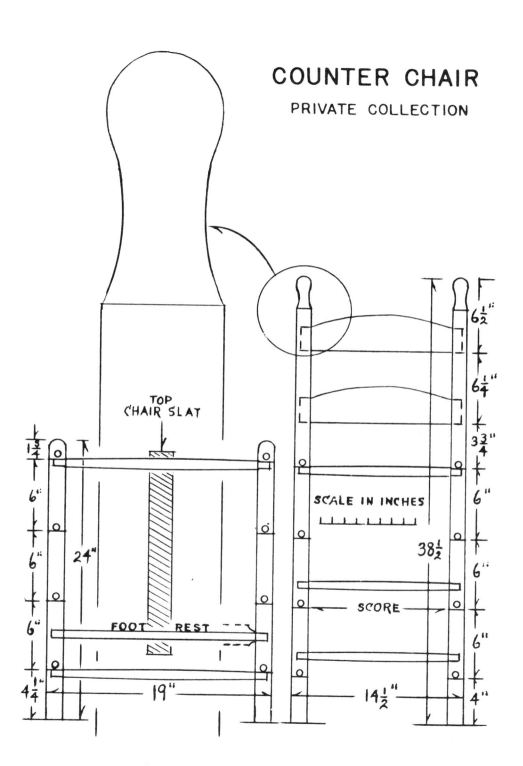

COUNTER CHAIR

PRIVATE COLLECTION

TOP
CHAIR SLAT

SCALE IN INCHES

$38\frac{1}{2}$

SCORE

FOOT REST

$6\frac{1}{2}$"

$6\frac{1}{4}$"

$3\frac{3}{4}$"

6"

6"

6"

4"

$1\frac{3}{4}$

6"

6"

24"

6"

$4\frac{1}{4}$"

19"

$14\frac{1}{2}$"

BRETHREN'S ROCKER
NEW LEBANON N.Y.

PRIVATE COLLECTION

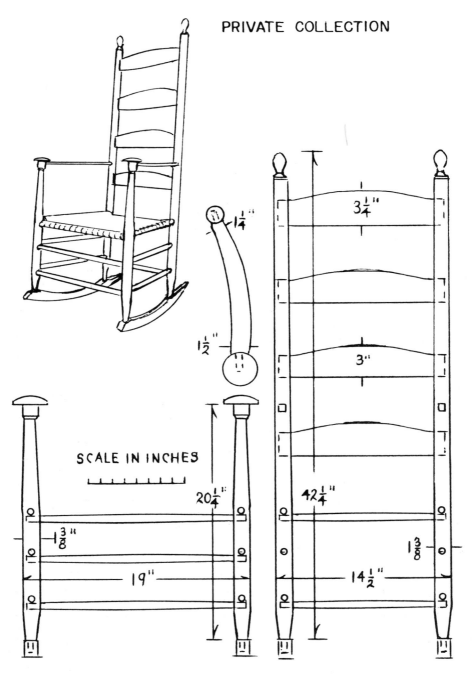

$1\frac{1}{4}$"

$1\frac{1}{2}$"

$3\frac{1}{4}$"

3"

$42\frac{1}{4}$"

$14\frac{1}{2}$"

$1\frac{3}{8}$"

SCALE IN INCHES

$20\frac{1}{4}$"

$1\frac{3}{8}$"

19"

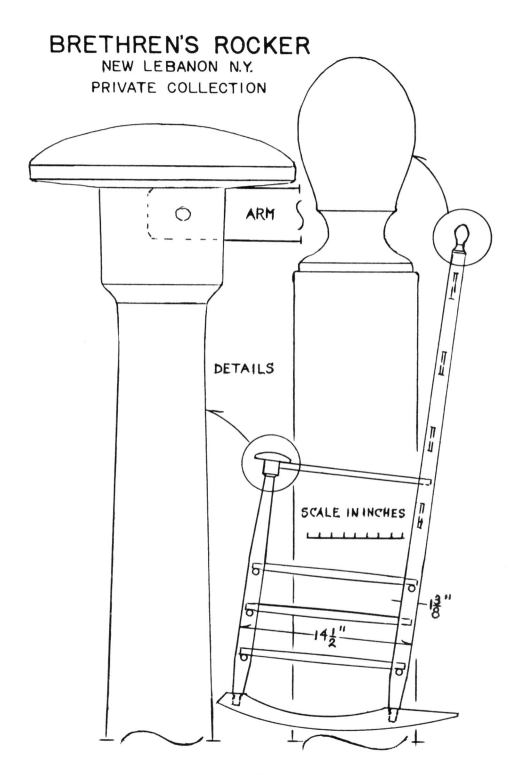

BRETHREN'S ROCKER
NEW LEBANON N.Y.
PRIVATE COLLECTION

ARM

DETAILS

SCALE IN INCHES

13¾"

14½"

CHAIR FINIALS

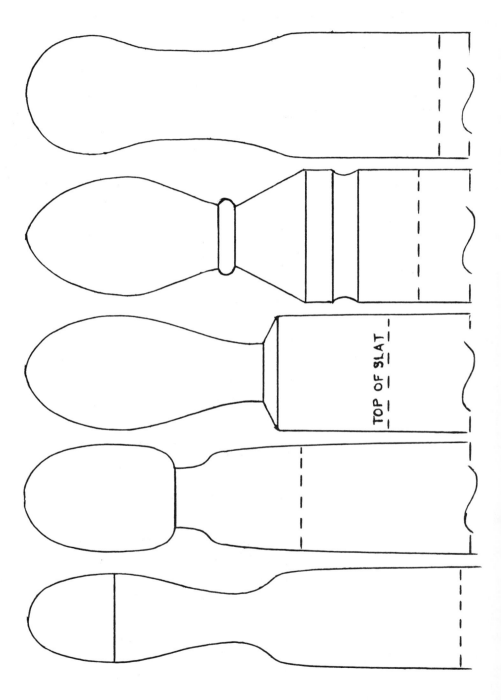

TOP OF SLAT

CHAIR MUSHROOMS
AND TILTING BUTTONS

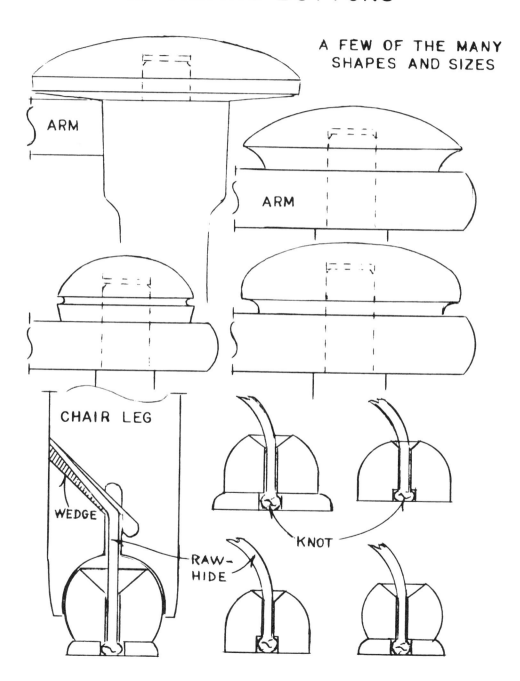

A FEW OF THE MANY
SHAPES AND SIZES

ARM

ARM

CHAIR LEG

WEDGE

RAW-
HIDE

KNOT

DRAWER PULLS

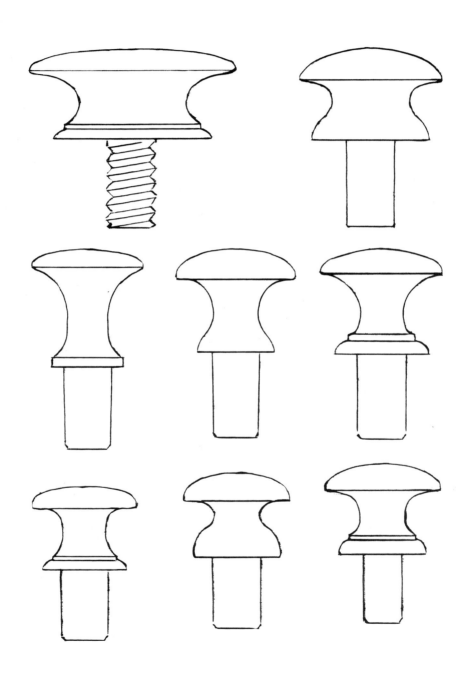

BED CASTERS

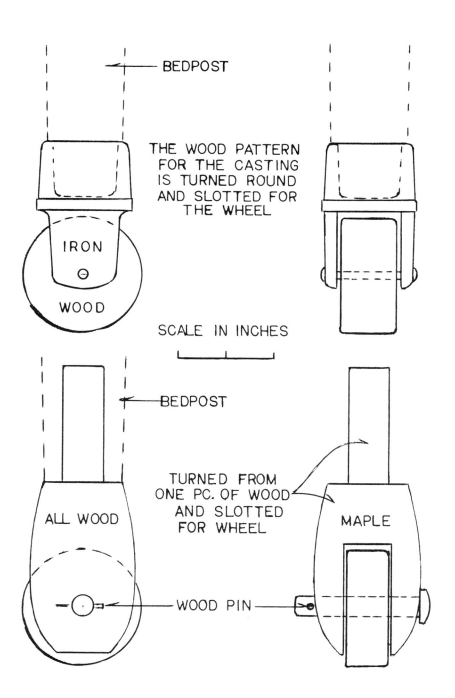

BEDPOST

THE WOOD PATTERN
FOR THE CASTING
IS TURNED ROUND
AND SLOTTED FOR
THE WHEEL

IRON

WOOD

SCALE IN INCHES

BEDPOST

TURNED FROM
ONE PC. OF WOOD
AND SLOTTED
FOR WHEEL

ALL WOOD

MAPLE

WOOD PIN

HANGING SHELF

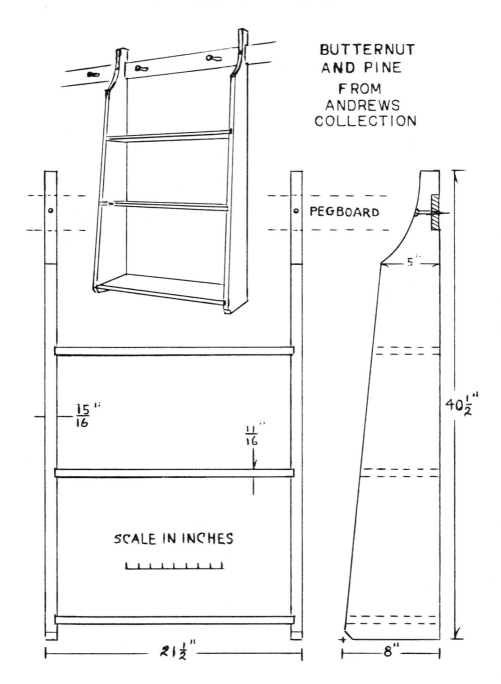

BUTTERNUT
AND PINE
FROM
ANDREWS
COLLECTION

PEGBOARD

5"

40½"

$\frac{15}{16}$"

$\frac{11}{16}$"

SCALE IN INCHES

21½"

8"

SMALL WALL CUPBOARD

HANCOCK SHAKER VILLAGE,
HANCOCK MASS.

DETAILS

PINE

$\frac{7}{16}" \times \frac{3}{4}"$ BATTENS

$11\frac{1}{8}"$

$4\frac{1}{2}"$

$\frac{1}{4}"$

$13"$

SCALE IN INCHES

$\frac{3}{8}"$

$\frac{1}{4}"$

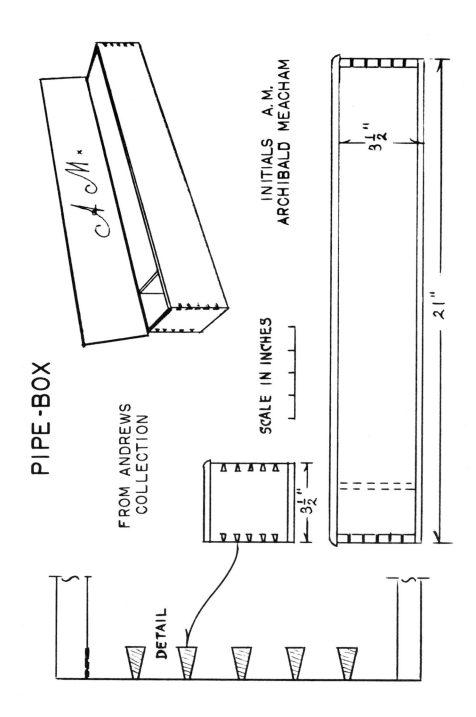

PIPE-BOX

FROM ANDREWS
COLLECTION

INITIALS A. M.
ARCHIBALD MEACHAM

SCALE IN INCHES

$3\frac{1}{2}$"

$3\frac{1}{2}$"

21"

DETAIL

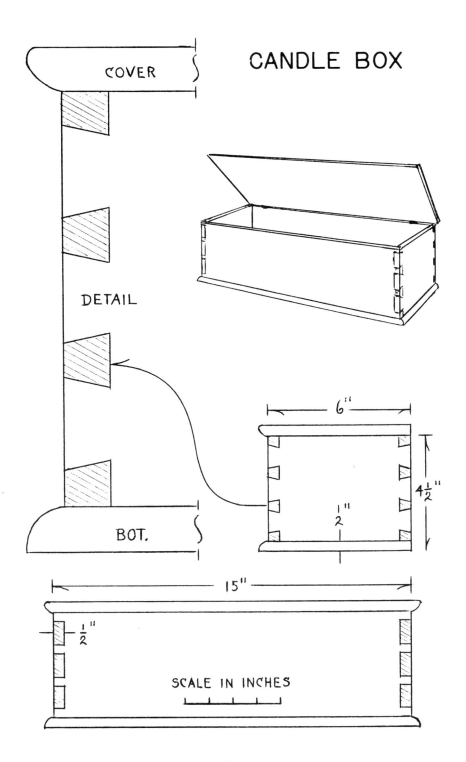

CANDLE BOX

COVER

DETAIL

BOT.

6"

4½"

½"

1"
2

15"

½"

SCALE IN INCHES

65

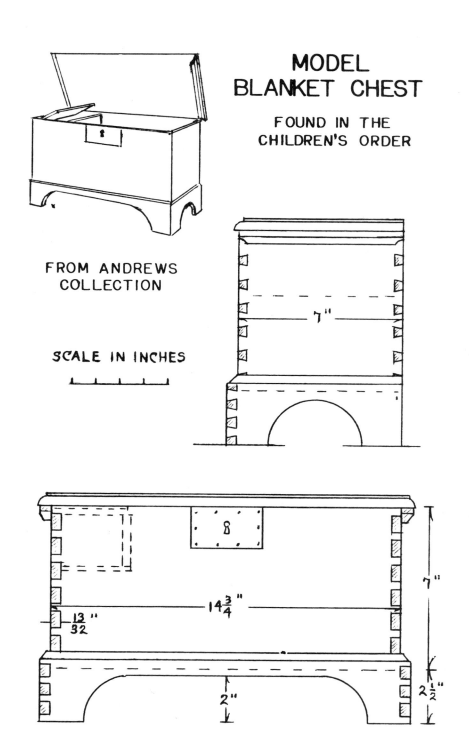

MODEL
BLANKET CHEST

FOUND IN THE
CHILDREN'S ORDER

FROM ANDREWS
COLLECTION

SCALE IN INCHES

7"

8

$14\frac{3}{4}$"

$\frac{13}{32}$"

7"

2"

$2\frac{1}{2}$"

WALNUT TRAY

NEW LEBANON, N.Y.   PRIVATE COLLECTION

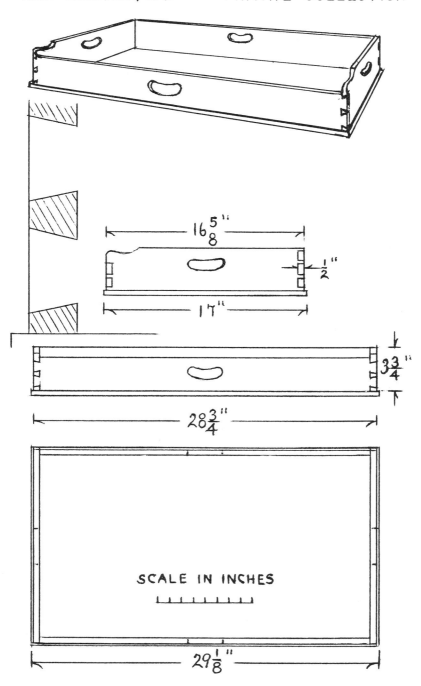

$16\frac{5}{8}''$

$\frac{1}{2}''$

$17''$

$3\frac{3}{4}''$

$28\frac{3}{4}''$

SCALE IN INCHES

$29\frac{1}{8}''$

SCOOP
PRIVATE COLLECTION

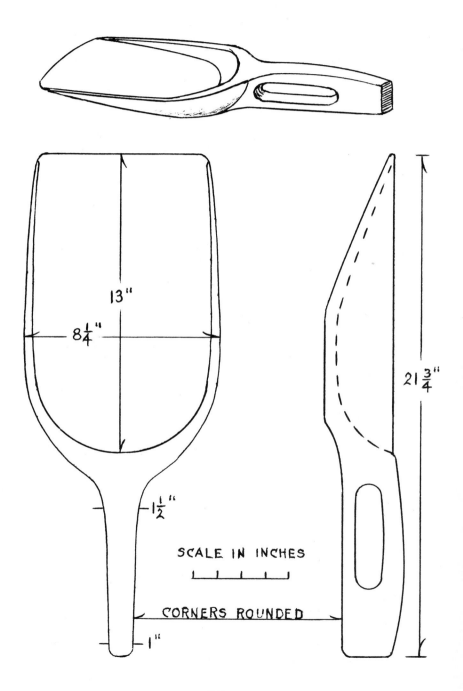

13"

$8\frac{1}{4}$"

$1\frac{1}{2}$"

$21\frac{3}{4}$"

SCALE IN INCHES

CORNERS ROUNDED

1"

MORTAR AND PESTLE
THE SHAKER MUSEUM, OLD CHATHAM, N.Y.

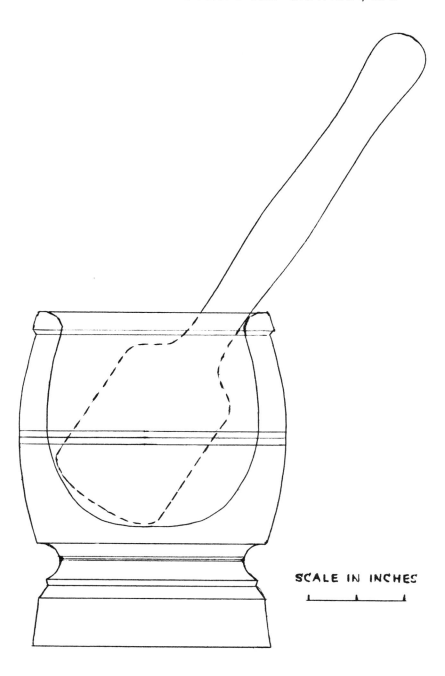

SCALE IN INCHES

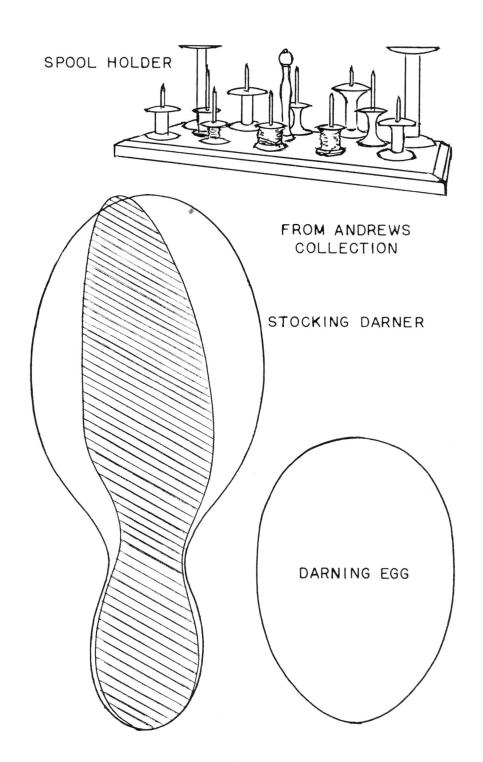

SPOOL HOLDER

FROM ANDREWS
COLLECTION

STOCKING DARNER

DARNING EGG

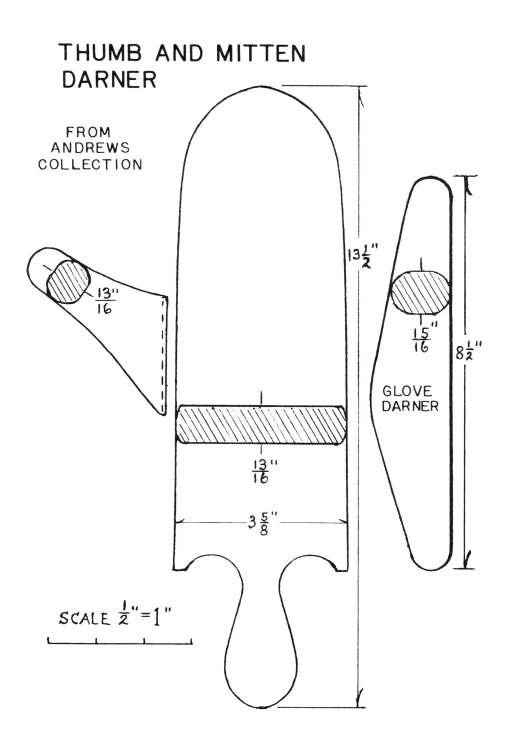

THUMB AND MITTEN DARNER

FROM
ANDREWS
COLLECTION

$\frac{13''}{16}$

$13\frac{1}{2}''$

$\frac{13''}{16}$

$3\frac{5}{8}''$

GLOVE
DARNER

$\frac{15''}{16}$

$8\frac{1}{2}''$

SCALE $\frac{1}{2}'' = 1''$

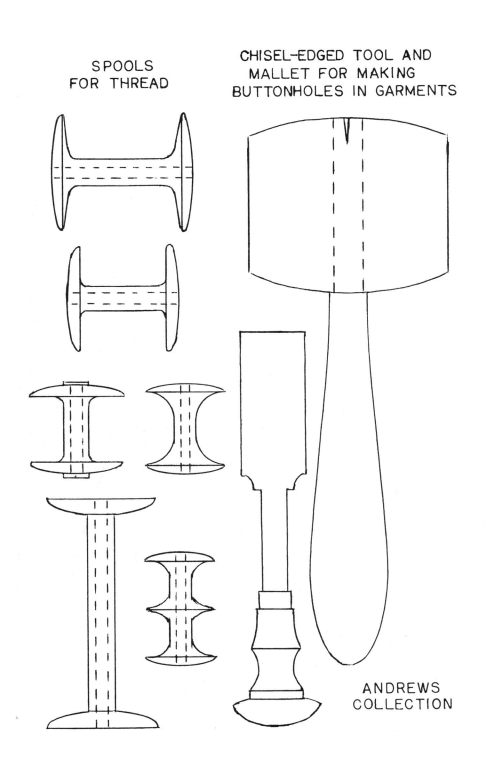

SPOOLS
FOR THREAD

CHISEL-EDGED TOOL AND
MALLET FOR MAKING
BUTTONHOLES IN GARMENTS

ANDREWS
COLLECTION

SHAKER MADE ITEMS

1 DARNER
2 BONNET PLEATER
3   "   "
4 SPOOL FOR THREAD

PRIVATE COLLECTION

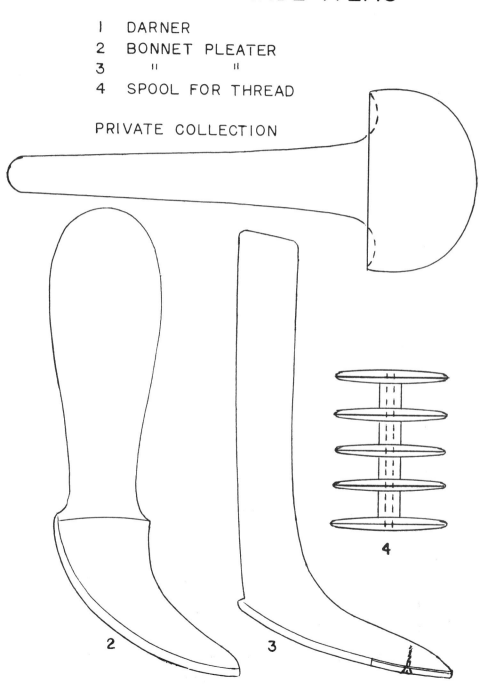

MT. LEBANON STOVE
DOUBLE FOR MORE EFFICIENT HEATING

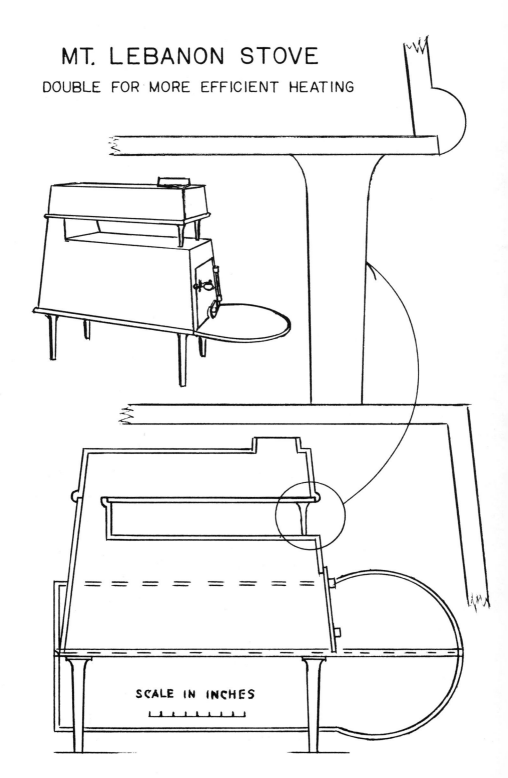

SCALE IN INCHES

MT. LEBANON STOVE

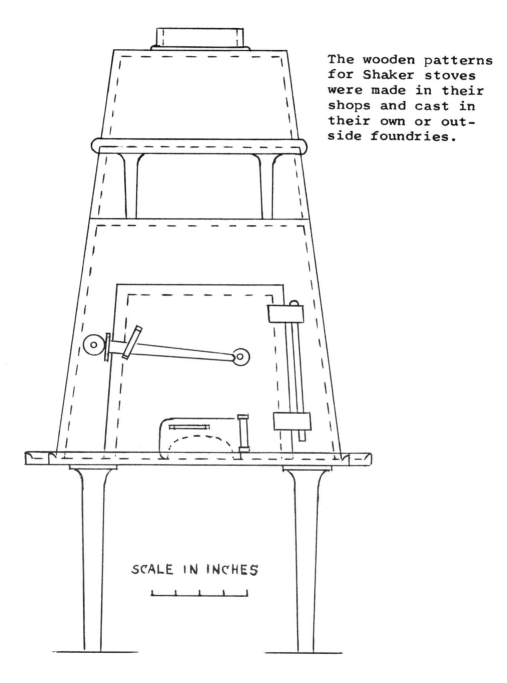

The wooden patterns
for Shaker stoves
were made in their
shops and cast in
their own or out-
side foundries.

SCALE IN INCHES

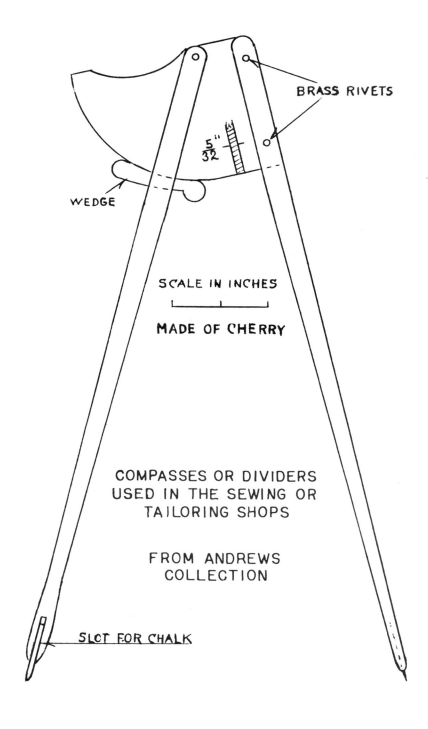

BRASS RIVETS

$\frac{5}{32}''$

WEDGE

SCALE IN INCHES

MADE OF CHERRY

COMPASSES OR DIVIDERS
USED IN THE SEWING OR
TAILORING SHOPS

FROM ANDREWS
COLLECTION

SLOT FOR CHALK

Brethren's Rocker — page 56

Washstand — page 33

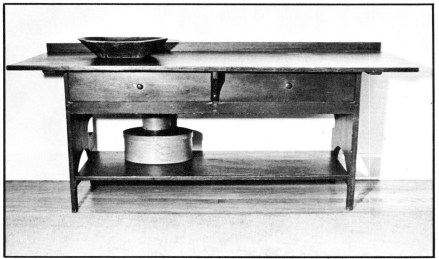

Bake-Room Table — page 16

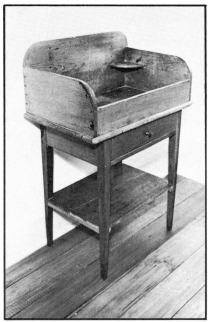

Washstand — page 30

Dividers — page 76

Drop-Leaf Table — page 18

Pine Table — page 14

Blanket Chest — page 34

Desk — page 4

Pine Bench — page 40

Loom Bench — page 42

Spool Holder — page 70

ABOUT THE AUTHOR

Ejner Handberg is a cabinetmaker of some 50 years experience. He was born in Denmark and came to the United States when he was 17 years old. He learned his craft from oldtime 19th century cabinet makers who insisted upon precision and accuracy.

A number of years ago he first became acquainted with the simplicity and dignity of Shaker furniture as a result of restoring and repairing many original pieces. His reputation in this field grew and the early collectors soon learned of his skill in such restorative work.

At this time, Ejner began to prepare meticulously perfect measured drawings of these original Shaker pieces for the purpose of reproducing them in his own shop one at a time. He made careful notes about the different types of wood used in the originals, and the unique methods of joining. He felt drawn to the basic Shaker designs that were characterized by the abolishment of non-essential ornamentations. He followed, as closely as possible, the reverence that these unusual people had for wood and the purely functional purpose in furniture.

This book, containing 80 of Mr. Handberg's carefully prepared scale drawings, represents much of his life's work. It includes drawings of Shaker chairs, tables, stands, sewing boxes, cupboards, desks, blanket chest and many other pieces.

The informed amateur worker in wood, as well as the professional cabinetmaker, will find Mr. Handberg's book a valuable addition to the perpetuation of Shaker qualities.

INDEX

Asterisks after plate numbers refer to drawings made from pieces in the collection of Dr. and Mrs. Edward Deming Andrews.